# Tudor Life

# WORK

## Paul Harrison

First published in 2009 by Wayland

Copyright © Wayland 2009

Wayland
338 Euston Road
London NW1 3BH

Wayland Australia
Level 17/207 Kent Street
Sydney NSW 2000

Senior Editor: Claire Shanahan
Designer: Jane Hawkins
Picture Researcher: Kathy Lockley

British Library Cataloguing in Publication Data
Harrison, Paul, 1969-
Work. - (Tudor life)
1. Occupations - England - History - 16th century -
Juvenile literature 2. England - Social conditions - 16th
century - Juvenile literature
 I. Title
331.7'00942'09031

ISBN 978 0 7502 5753 4

Picture acknowledgements: The Board of Trustees
of the Armouries (Institution Reference: 1-196-862) /
Heritage-Images: 5, 12, 12CR, The Board of Trustees
of the Armouries/HIP/TopFoto/TopFoto.com: 13, The
Berger Collection at the Denver Art Museum, USA/Getty
Images: 23, Mike Booth/Alamy: 11, British Library, London,
UK/©British Library Board. All Rights   Reserved/Bridgeman
Art Library, London: 4, 15, Mary Evans Photo Library: 21, Mary
Evans Picture Library/Alamy: 17, geogphotos/Alamy: 25, Glasgow
University Library, Scotland/Bridgeman Art Library, London: 19,
Guildhall Art Gallery, City of London/Bridgeman Art Library/Getty Images:
16, Hulton Archive/Getty Images: 12BL, INTERFOTO pressebildagentur/Alamy: title page, 9,
10, Kunsthistorisches Museum, Vienna, Austria/Bridgeman Art Library/Getty Images: 14, 28,
Lebrecht Music & Fine Arts Photo Library/Alamy: 20, Philippa Lewis; Edifice/Corbis: 22,
Pawel Libera/Corbis: 6, London Art Archive/Alamy: 24, North Wind Pictures/Alamy: COVER
(Main), 27, Palazzo Barberini, Rome, Italy/Bridgeman Art Library/Getty Images: 8, The Print
Collector/Alamy: COVER (inset), 18, Private Collection/Bridgeman Art Library, London: 26
Society of Antiquaries, London, UK/Bridgeman Art Library/Getty Images: 7

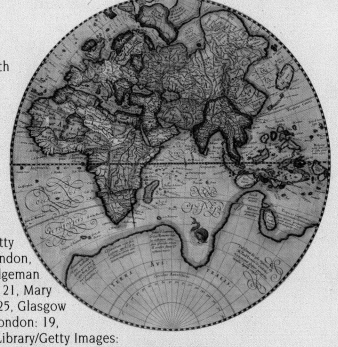

Printed in China

Wayland is a division of Hachette Children's Books, an Hachette UK company.
www.hachettelivre.co.uk

# Contents

Words in **bold** can be found
in the glossary.

# Toil and turmoil

The Tudor family ruled England from 1485, when Henry Tudor defeated King Richard III at the Battle of Bosworth Field to become King Henry VII. Tudor rule ended when Elizabeth I died in 1603, leaving no heir to take over from her.

## Turmoil and triumph

During the reign of the Tudors, the country suffered wars, **famine**, plague and religious change. However, there were also great voyages of discovery by explorers and new countries were colonised. The arts, such as music and painting, were encouraged. Plays were also popular during the Tudor period and theatres such as the Globe were built in London.

A recreation of the Globe theatre was built in 1997 on the site of the original theatre.

# A changing country

At the start of the Tudor period, most people lived in the countryside and worked on the land – either on their own farms or as labourers for someone else. However, towns and cities, especially London, were growing quickly. More and more people moved to towns to find work doing jobs that didn't exist in the countryside, such as shopkeeping.

## Henry VII
## 1457–1509

Henry Tudor was born in Wales in 1457, but spent much of his childhood in France. At the time, England was split, with rival families claiming the throne in a civil war called the **Wars of the Roses**. When Henry became king, much of his time was taken up with keeping the country at peace. He made it illegal for powerful families to have their own armies and also signed peace treaties with England's rival, France.

King Henry VII made England a wealthy country after years of war.

# The Royal Court

It was the **monarch**'s job to run the country. They made laws, raised money through taxes, and decided if the country should go to war with another country.

## Always on call

The monarch's day was often spent appearing at the Royal Court. It was here that the day-to-day running of the country and its affairs were carried out, and disputes settled. Here the king or queen was surrounded by **courtiers**, nobles, **bishops**, ministers and lawyers who were there to ask questions or offer advice. Representatives from foreign countries, called ambassadors, would also visit the Court to discuss issues between their country and England.

One of the most famous of the Tudor rulers was King Henry VIII, who ruled from 1509–1547.

8

# Close advisers

The monarch relied upon a close band of advisers called the Privy Council to help him make decisions. One of the most important members of the Council was the Master of the Stool, because he was with the monarch more than most. Unfortunately, he also had one of the worst jobs – it was his task to wipe the monarch's bottom!

Henry VIII surrounded by the Privy Council, which was made up of about 40 men in the 1540s.

## Sir Christopher Hatton, 1540–1591

Sir Christopher Hatton held one of the most important jobs in the country. He was Lord Chancellor when the last Tudor monarch, Elizabeth I, was on the throne. The Chancellor appointed judges and made sure the law courts were fair. It was said that Hatton was an excellent dancer and that the Queen gave him a job as she was so impressed with his footwork.

# Downstairs staff

During the Tudor period, wealthy people and nobles lived in big houses with large grounds. These needed an army of servants to run properly, so thousands of people were employed in large households across the country.

 Kitchen staff in nobles' houses were expected to feed over 1,000 people if the Royal Court visited.

## Helping hand

Not all Tudor servants were from poor backgrounds. Noblemen often sent their sons and daughters to work for other nobles as a part of their education. Usually these well-off servants would train as secretaries, helping the noblemen with their paperwork and the running of their estates.

## Servants

It was the steward's job to organise the servants. Stewards were educated men and helped run the household. The other servants would usually be men and they would do a variety of jobs, from cleaning to serving at table. A servant's day would often start at four o'clock in the morning and finish only when the master of the house and his guests had retired for the night.

This photo is from a historical recreation at Hampton Court Palace. It shows the typical clothes worn by a male servant, which were provided by the master of the house.

## Worst job

The worst jobs went to the youngest members of staff. Young boys, called scullions, did most of the scrubbing and washing up, often when everyone else – including the other servants – had gone to bed. When the scullion had finished, he was often left to sleep on the kitchen floor.

## Written at the time

Many Tudors believed that they had a fixed place in society, as the *First Book of Homilies* (1547) explains:

'Every degree of people ... hath appointed to them their duty and order: some are in high degree, some in low; some Kings and Princes, some Inferiors and Subjects; Priests and Laymen, Masters and Servants, Fathers and Children, Husbands and Wives, Rich and Poor: and everyone hath need of other.'

# Men at arms

For most of the Tudor period, there were few full-time soldiers. Instead, every man was expected to train as a soldier for a few days each year and be ready to join the army to protect the country if needed.

## A hard life

Life in the army was terribly hard. The food was awful, the discipline was harsh, and often the soldiers were ill-equipped, with little or no armour to protect them. On top of all this, the organisation of the army was so poor that the soldiers' wages were usually late and sometimes not paid at all!

This gun was made in Germany in 1537 for King Henry VIII. ⇨

### A Tudor object

Hand-held guns became more popular during the Tudor period. This gun was specially made for Henry VIII. It is called a breech-loading matchlock. This means the shot was put into the back of the gun (the breech) along with gunpowder. The powder was lit with a slow-burning match (the matchlock) to fire the gun. It is decorated with a picture of a Tudor rose – a symbol of the Tudor family.

⇦ Mons Meg was one of the largest Tudor cannons ever made. It can be seen today at Edinburgh castle.

# Paid to fight

Although Englishmen had to defend their country, they were not expected to travel abroad to fight in wars. The monarch had to persuade people to fight, but it was often difficult to find enough people to join up. For many men sent to fight abroad, it was the first time they had been away from their village, never mind travel to a different country. Instead, some soldiers were hired from other countries to fight for the English. This type of soldier is called a **mercenary**.

During the Tudor years of 1485–1603, England went to war against Scotland, Ireland, France, Spain and the Dutch.

# Explorers and sailors

A powerful country needed a strong navy – both warships for protection and **merchant** ships for **trade**. Tudor explorers discovered new lands to **colonise** in the name of the monarch, while warships guarded **trade routes** and defended England from attack.

Sir Francis Drake (1540–1595) captained the first English ship to sail around the world. ⬇

## Off to sea

Both rich and poor people went to work at sea. Men from noble families became captains while the poor became common sailors or soldiers. Even children worked on ships – often to carry gunpowder from the magazine to the cannons.

## Cramped conditions

Life on board was harsh and cramped. For example, the *Mary Rose* carried over 400 soldiers and sailors. Work never stopped on a ship. Decks had to be washed to stop them from drying out and splitting, and ropes had to be repaired and sails constantly adjusted.

# On-board diet

Ships could be away for years at a time and the diet was poor. There were no refrigerators, so fresh meat was covered in salt to stop it from going bad. Even water went stale after a while, so sailors drank weak beer instead. There was little fresh fruit or vegetables, so sailors often suffered from a disease called **scurvy**.

⬇ Geradus Mercator (1512–1594) was a Flemish man who started his work on country and world maps in the 1530s.

## A Tudor object

The Mercator map was a great aid to Tudor sailors. Getting lost when sailing was a big hazard. Crews could starve to death if their ship missed land, so knowing where you were was very important. The Mercator maps were very accurate which allowed sailors to plot a true course for their vessels when exploring or in battle.

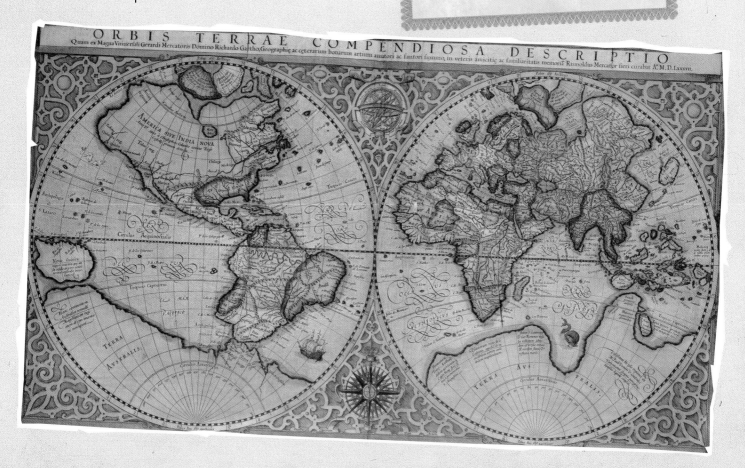

# Religion

At the centre of Tudor life was religion. The working day started with prayers and, by Queen Elizabeth I's reign, everyone was forced to go to church by law. People in **religious orders**, such as priests, were important members of the community.

## Religious duties

Priests were often educated and respected men. Apart from holding church services and **baptising**, marrying and burying their **parishioners**, priests also taught the children of wealthy families. Priests, monks and nuns also looked after poor people in the local area.

### Cardinal Thomas Wolsey, 1475–1530

A religious life could allow people from humble backgrounds to become very important people. Thomas Wolsey was the son of a butcher, but rose through different jobs in the Church to become an important official known as a Cardinal. Wolsey was also one of Henry VIII's most trusted advisors and the King made Wolsey his Lord Chancellor. However, he eventually displeased Henry and was arrested for treason. Wolsey died on his way to prison.

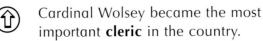

Cardinal Wolsey became the most important **cleric** in the country.

## Religious excesses

However, not all religious figures were popular. Occasionally, bishops and **friars** became exceedingly wealthy, spending more time eating, drinking and generally enjoying themselves at the Royal Court, than looking after their priests and monks.

## Witchcraft

The Tudors had many **superstitions** and believed in magic. Some women called themselves 'cunning women' or witches. They travelled from village to village selling charms. Although many people were happy to go to church as well as visit a cunning woman, being a witch was actually illegal. If a witch was caught by the authorities, she was likely to be executed.

A suspected witch is ducked into the river. It was thought that, if she drowned, she was innocent and, if she survived, she was guilty and would be executed.

# An educated life

A good education, for those who could afford it, was the way to get a good job. Some of the best jobs were in law and many young men studied to become lawyers. However, there were many other respectable professions to choose from.

## Law and order

One of the most important people in any English county was the Justice of the Peace. He was the monarch's representative and made sure people were doing what the monarch wanted. It was also the Justice of the Peace's job to keep law and order, run the local courts, and even arrange the repair of local roads and bridges.

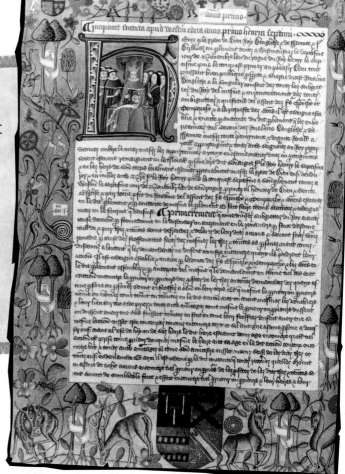

### A Tudor object

This document is an act of parliament – a new law that has been passed by the government and the monarch. This one dates from 1485 and declares Henry VII to be the rightful King of England. When the monarch passed a new law, it was up to the Justices of the Peace to make sure the common people heard about it and, more importantly, followed it.

This act of parliament has a portrait of Henry VII (top, left) and a decorated border of plants and flowers.

## The educators

Anyone could set up their own school to teach young children how to read, but one of the better teaching jobs was to be a personal tutor to a nobleman's children. Universities were popular, too, and many men worked as tutors there.

## Bad medicine

Sometimes, even the best Tudor education wasn't good enough to do certain jobs properly. For example, doctors believed animal dung was useful as medicine, and surgery was generally carried out by barbers!

Tudor doctors were eager to learn more about the human body. This illustration shows John Banister, a famous anatomist, giving a lecture to student doctors in about 1580.

# An urban life

Towns and cities grew bigger during the Tudor period because they were centres of **trade** – where people brought goods to sell or send abroad. Towns also attracted people who were looking for work.

London almost trebled in size during the Tudor period. By 1600, there were over 200,000 people living there.

## Time for trade

England became wealthy through trade with foreign countries. Cloth and wool were in big demand from abroad, as well as coal, tin and lead. A merchant would buy these goods and then sell them on to different countries. With new colonies springing up in America, this was a good time for merchants and many of them became rich.

## Making and selling

Another feature of towns and cities were the craftsmen and shopkeepers. Makers of luxury items such as **goldsmiths** and **silversmiths** were attracted by the wealth found in the city. Everyday objects such as bowls or tools were also made inside the city, or close by – either to be traded abroad or sold at home.

Goldsmiths, shown here in 1568, produced a variety of objects, from cups and chalices to rings, seals and crowns. These were, mainly for the monarch, the Church and wealthy people.

## Support staff

Most people in towns were not merchants or skilled workers. Instead, many were employed in physical jobs, such as portering – the carrying of goods from **quaysides** and businesses. Water travel was also important, especially in London, and ferrymen rowed customers up and down the River Thames.

21

# A rural life

Most Tudor people lived and worked in the country. Many people rented land that they farmed for themselves. Poor people worked as labourers for wealthy people on their large estates or on big farms belonging to **yeomen**.

Yeomen often built fine houses from brick with glazed windows, like this one. Labourers had to make do with draughty homes made of rushes.

## Out in the fields

Whether you were a yeoman, a farmer or a labourer, the work in the fields depended on the season. During the lighter summer months, country people would rise at four o'clock, but during the winter this could be as late as five. All work was done by hand, be it **sowing** or **harvesting** crops, **ploughing** fields or even spreading manure!

## Farm animals

Looking after farm animals was a vital job as animals not only provided food to eat but did all the heavy work done by machines today. Horses or oxen were used for ploughing and they needed feeding several times a day, as well as mucking out.

## The poor

Labourers were paid in food and small amounts of money. It was an uncertain life – if the harvest was poor they often starved. Some tried moving to the city while others simply became beggars.

⬆ Harvesting crops was tiring, dusty and back-breaking work.

## Written at the time

This Tudor law described how long a farm labourer should work each day:

'[A] labourer shall be at work ... before five of the clock in the morning. And that he have but half an hour for his breakfast and an hour and a half for his dinner ... and that he depart not from his work till between seven and eight of the clock in the evening.'

# Second-class citizens

In Tudor times, women were not thought to be as important as men. However, this did not stop women from working or holding positions of great responsibility.

## Wealthy and powerful

Running the great Tudor estates was considered to be a man's job, but it was the wives of noblemen who actually did it, as their husbands were often away at Court. Tudor women could be rich in their own right, but they were expected to hand over all of their wealth to their husbands when they married.

### Queen Elizabeth I, 1533–1603

There were three Tudor queens on the English throne. Elizabeth I was the first Tudor queen and she reigned for 45 years, during a time of great exploration and relative calm at home. As a noblewoman she was highly educated, and she proved to be an intelligent and charming leader. She never married or produced an heir and so was the last of the Tudor monarchs.

 A portrait of Queen Elizabeth I at the time of her coronation in 1559.

⬆ Making and mending clothes was all part of a woman's work in the home.

## At home

Being a housewife was one of the busiest jobs in Tudor Britain. Much of a housewife's time was spent in the kitchen as everything that was eaten or drunk had to be made by hand. A housewife also had to raise the children and clean the house. No surprise that her work often started before four o'clock in the morning.

## On the farm

In the countryside, women were expected to help out around the farm with jobs such as killing and plucking poultry, or bringing in the harvest. Farmers' wives also had to feed animals and milk cows daily, and grow herbs and vegetables.

# Childhood

A Tudor childhood was short and hard. Around half of all children died of disease or starvation before they turned seven years old. Many poor children were working by that age and girls might be married by the age of 14.

## Hard lessons

Usually only the male children of wealthy families went to school – girls were taught at home if at all. Pupils went to school six days a week and the school day started as early as six in the morning and lasted for up to ten hours! Pupils learned Latin and other languages, and sometimes mathematics.

To complete a wealthy child's education, they were sent into the service of a nobleman. There they also learned various sports and pastimes, as well as how to behave in society. When this was complete, the young man would go on to university.

Beatings were common in Tudor schools.

# Written at the time

Roger Ascham, Elizabeth I's tutor, describes what the son of a wealthy noble might learn in his book the *The Schoolmaster*, written in 1570:

'... to ride comely, to run fair at the tilt or ring, to play at all weapons, to shoot fair with the bow or surely in gun, to vault lustily, to run, to leap, to wrestle, to swim, to dance comely, to sing and play of instruments cunningly, to hawk, to hunt, to play at tennis and all pastimes generally which be ... fit exercise for war or some pleasant pastime for peace.'

## Young workers

Poor male children went to work. This work might be in the form of an **apprenticeship** – learning a trade by working for a craftsman, such as a silversmith. This often meant leaving home and going to live with the master from whom they were learning. An apprenticeship lasted for around seven years.

➡️ A master was responsible for the moral upbringing of their apprentices as well as their education.

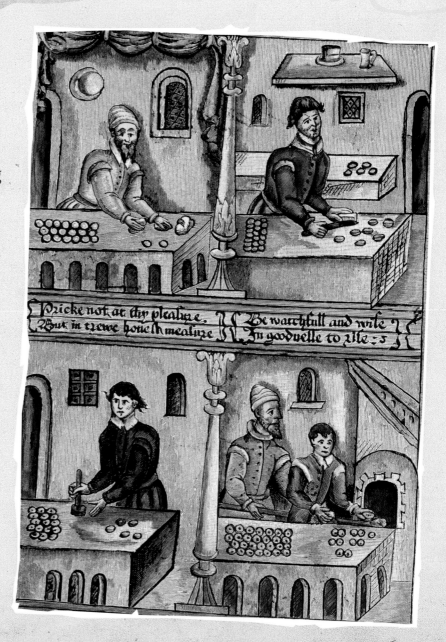

# Timeline

| | |
|---|---|
| 1485 | King Henry VII takes the throne after the Battle of Bosworth Field. The start of the Tudor period. |
| 1487 | The official end of the Wars of the Roses. |
| 1492 | Christopher Columbus sails to the West Indies to explore. |
| 1509 | Henry VII dies and Henry VIII becomes king. |
| 1515 | Cardinal Wolsey becomes Lord Chancellor. |
| 1519 | The Portuguese explorer Ferdinand Magellan becomes the first person to sail around the world. |
| 1535 | Wales becomes part of the Kingdom of England. |
| 1545 | The *Mary Rose* sinks. |
| 1547 | Henry VIII dies and Edward VI comes to the throne. |
| 1553 | King Edward VI dies. Lady Jane Grey takes the throne for nine days. Mary I comes to the throne. |
| 1558 | Mary I dies and Elizabeth I comes to the throne. |
| 1577 | Sir Francis Drake sails around the world. |
| 1584 | Sir Walter Raleigh sets up a colony in Virginia, America. |
| 1588 | The defeat of the Spanish Armada. |
| 1590s | The first Shakespeare plays are performed. |
| 1599 | The Globe theatre is built. |
| 1603 | Queen Elizabeth I dies leaving no heir, marking the end of the Tudor period. |

# Glossary

**apprenticeship** a period of time when a child learns a trade

**baptising** part of a ceremony to welcome a parishioner into a particular religion

**bishops** a high ranking cleric of a church

**cleric** an appointed member of a church such as a priest or vicar

**colonise** where one country rules part of a different country and builds their own settlements there

**courtier** a member of the Royal Court

**famine** a long period of time when food is in short supply

**friars** a member of a religious order

**goldsmiths** craftsmen that work with gold

**harvesting** collecting in the ripe crops

**monarch** the ruler of a country

**mercenary** a soldier who is paid to fight for an army other than that of his own country

**merchant** a person who sells goods for profit. Especially used for people who trade with othtr countries

**parishioners** The people who go to a particular church

**ploughing** digging over the soil with a long blade called a plough which is pulled by horses or oxen

**quaysides** the area where ships and boats are loaded and unloaded

**religious orders** Groups of people who devote their lives to God, such as monks and nuns

**silversmiths** craftsmen that work with silver

**sowing** planting crops

**superstitions** a belief in magic and unknown powers

**trade** the exchange of goods prodrouce for money, or for other goods

**trade routes** paths from one country to another often used for transporting goods

**Wars of the Roses** a series of battles between the Houses of York and Lancaster for the English throne that lasted from 1455 to 1487

**yeomen** low-ranking officials, or attendants of the monarch

# Index

# Resources

*People in the Past:* *Tudor Jobs* Haydn Middleton, Heinemann, 2003

*Who Was Henry VIII?* Kay Barnham, Wayland 2007

*http://www.channel4.com/history/microsites/W/worstjobs/tudor1.html*
Describes the worst jobs in Tudor times.

*hhttp://www.nmm.ac.uk/TudorExploration/NMMHTML/html/on_seas.html*
Find out more about Tudor sailors and ships.